To

Nerrie

I wish you a wonderful
Christmas with your
daughter and family.
I hope you enjoy this
read.

lots of love,

Vicky, Giorgio &
zen oo

xxdd
x

# The Winter Hedge

## Walks in a Deep Lane

ex libris

Candlestick Press

Published by:
Candlestick Press,
Diversity House, 72 Nottingham Road, Arnold, Nottingham NG5 6LF
www.candlestickpress.co.uk

Design and typesetting by Craig Twigg

Printed by Bayliss Printing Company Ltd of Worksop, UK

Donation to the Woodland Trust
www.woodlandtrust.org.uk

ISBN 978 1 913627 32 4

**Acknowledgements**

Katharine Towers 'Hedge' first published here by kind permission of the author.

Where poets are no longer living, their dates are given.

# Contents

"Vital features in the landscape, hedges are more than an essential refuge for wildlife. Small but mighty, they also clean our air, capture carbon (and) reduce flooding..."

*The Woodland Trust*

## Hedge

No place to shelter or hide in
but a field is spoken for

follow one bent twig
gold in lichen

back to the branch
back to the mother-stem

and to the mother's mother
to find an almost-end

the blunt old rootstock
furnishing the dark


*Katharine Towers*

# The Winter Hedge
*Walks in a Deep Lane*

The sky over the valley was grey and the pasture crisp with frost. I didn't feel like being out this early, but the dog wanted walking so we went down into the deep lane. He trotted over the cobbles, nose alive with scents. I followed behind. A particular light seeped over the hedges, a leafless gleam jostling with the wind. Beyond the woody elbows of hazel and hawthorn, among burdock and spiderwebs, a stream slithered in the ditch. As we went on, it gathered strength from the springs in the hillside and flowed more freely. I've spied signs of otters here before, but it's so shallow, there can't be much for them to eat.

Round a corner, over a fallen tree, and an old crow eyed us, guarding the ribs of a dead rabbit. We went deeper down, into the tunnel of bare hazel. There were pools in the mud, catching the glisten of something, an ancient wolf-light, a grizzled bridge through time. This valley has been here longer than people have. It was worn by meltwater as the planet released the land from its weight of ice. People came later, looking for fresh water, good hunting and shelter. They built these earth banks, made these hedges and ditches, as if they were promises against winter starvation.

The lane made a curve and a dip, and the dog's nose picked up a trail: the deer had been here moments before, their slots hurrying through the grass and brambles. The sun sent weak rays through the bare willows on the bank of the stream. Something was tense. Not deer, they had vanished. A grey heron, motionless, waiting for something, anything to eat. The bird shifted from its hunched stance, lengthening its neck by increments as it moved. I thought of my yoga class, where with bare feet you lengthen and stretch, open the spaciousness between each winter-stiff bone. Tree. Mountain. Warrior. The stealth-white neck lifted, its tattered flecks positioning the yellow-dagger bill.

# The lane tasted of frost, cold as starlight

When there's a cold-snap it can be easy for herons to perish, but this creature is versatile. I once spotted one standing priest-like around the mole hills, and when I trespassed into the field I found the prey remains compressed into a pellet of fur — the bleached bones and tiny incisors of a young mole.

The lane tasted of frost, cold as starlight. Shivers of ice had formed on leaf edges and reeds. A wren's frantic calls: the quick chink-chink-chink gave away their alarm at me and the dog. Leaf-brown, the bird flicked through the hedge, along branches and over stones, mouse-like. It's the anxious up-tick tail that makes this winter bird unique. The tiny king of birds is a druid in old stories, singing out in midwinter. It was hunted and sacrificed each year, but most of all right now, it showed that there were still insects to eat. It flickered down, picked at little morsels, juicy spiders perhaps.

You can tell the age of a hedgerow by the number of species that survive there. Thirty metres of hedge might contain seven trees and on those many more species live: lichens, liverworts and mosses, and hundreds of fungi beneath that. But the density of insect life amongst it all makes the hedge most astounding: the pollarded ash and cut hawthorn, the woven hazel, field maple, oak; all the plants provide thousands of insect species with food and shelter. In amongst the sycamores' slick of fallen leaves and composting earth were slugs, snails and earthworms. This was the mulch of "honest rot" that Sylvia Plath found in her 'November Graveyard'. For Plath the ebbing light of winter could unpick the heart, but inside my hedge was the gleam of a thousand living creatures. Larvae and sheltering moths, secret constellations of life beneath the surface. Creatures of the night. The nut tree tussock moth, the magpie moth, the chequered fruit tree tortrix, the scalloped hazel.

In amongst the earthy cocoons, microscopic spores of fungi, and beneath these, the sickly-sweet scent of mycorrhizal tendrils, crushed and exposed by digging badgers, or spread by fox fur, or tangled between the spines of wintering hedgehogs.

I brushed the reptilian curls of bracken and they breathed out spiced-leather scents, leaf litter, oak galls. Deeper down, layers of bones; generations of passing away, a captured pattern telling of musky, gentle death.

Close to the old mill, hidden right at the end of the track, a wisp of smoke rose. The comforting aroma of cut wood and fuel gathered in, the tannin of fresh wood stacks and the waft of woodsmoke is conjured by John Clare: "I love to see the cottage smoke / Curl upwards through the naked trees / The pigeons nestled round the coat / On November days like these". The smell of kindled hearths goes all the way into the core of you.

**Among the dreaming skeletons of hazel and ash**

In the evening I walked again into the deep lane. This time brought the chill spectre of the moon. In the night air I gazed at its strange dazzle through a veil of cloud. Time was passing, its wintery tides drawing us inward, to gather our forces for the harsh season. RS 'Sam' Gwynn pinpoints it: "For all that lags and eases, all that shows / The winding-downward and diminished scale / Of days declining to a twilit chill, / Breathe quietly, release into repose: / Be still".

The hedge's oak, field maple and hazel may have given up their leaves but running through, grasping the exposed, gnarly trunks was a profusion of deep green ivy. This plant is the softer side of the holly and ivy duo. We gather the feminine ivy to weave circular wreaths, to decorate our houses at Yuletide. With a green that defies death, in the centre of winter, she is the promise of unquenchable life. The masculine spikes of holly can grow alongside ivy, but lean in and listen to their difference.

Holly fights with the wind, while the ivy gently clatters with it, celebrating. Ivy is the more magical of the two. Her twining growth and enveloping leaves offer insulation and harbour for insects and birds. The smothering habit is not as dangerous as we think. Ivy is about protection. She maintains natural balance in the hedge. The hard, black calorie-rich berries are less glamorous than the blood-red holly berries, but they are food-a-plenty for wintering song thrushes, mistle thrushes, blackbirds, redwings and blackcaps. A wry old tradition warns: whichever plant is brought into the house first predicts whether the man or the woman of the house will rule that year. Cut your ivy sparingly at the solstice and revive that tradition, but go for equality, and remember to leave some for the birds.

## Moments of restful dark

At the nadir of the year after the darkness we see the sun returning through the woven tunnel of the green lane. With the gift of its sparse light you can experience the smaller splendours now. These moments of restful dark around the waning year are the source of rebirth. "And like seeds dreaming beneath the snow, your heart dreams of spring," Kahlil Gibran tells us.

As my feet made their way along the muddy contours, as I trod my way downward, in among the dreaming skeletons of hazel and ash, hibernation was all around; life retracted to its centre. People sometimes come down here on bikes, but you miss everything at mud-splattering speed. Rosy-purple twigs of dogwood, sleeping moths amongst the towering beauty of oaks, bark textures fresh and bare, lifting your mood, twig by knotty twig. Black ash knuckles. King Alfred's cakes. Hart's tongue ferns. The earth smells of old thorns, dog rose and ropes of dried honeysuckle; foxglove leaves, old dandelion, a concoction and mesh of wintering foliage. When it emerges anew, the common foxglove will create spires of purple, loved by bees but toxic to humans. On the other hand following the diagnosis of heart failure it can increase blood flow, and slow and strengthen the heartbeat, though this is not to be tried at home. In the hedge is medicine.

The sky darkened and a soft, cold rain began to fall. The tentative drops were a massage for the scalp, and balm for the inner ear. With rasping calls that echoed over the treetops the old crow circled, looking down on our small figures, dog and person, washed by the rain. The path became a rusty stream, and left us with only the water-worn elementals: Wood. Earth. Rock. "With an eye made quiet by the power / of harmony, and the deep power of joy / we see into the life of things," Wordsworth said. He knew how the blood pressure softened, the pulse gentled the soul open.

**A final treasury of glints**

The special flora of ancient hedges is still dormant in January, and beneath the bracken and leaf litter the wood sorrel, bluebell and wild garlic are wrapped in roots and earth, waiting.

A new morning, and an easterly had brought a hard frost to coat everything. The glassy film of ice lingered in root clefts and rock pockets all day amongst the hedge's shadows and surfaces.

A quick bright movement and my mouth formed the word 'stoat' almost before I'd thought it. Its white throat and chestnut back sleek as fire, it was a speed-stripe, streaked with winter. Over the twigs and branches, its surge was a spool of hunger. It melted me to a steaming breath.

Hedges mesh animals to the land, their seasonal witness of small migrations, wild, domestic and human as they travel, seeking cover, water and safe browsing. These muscular ways are long enough to stretch to the moon and back and yet inside there is intimacy. In a nook I found a sheltering place, where you could crawl in among the roots. I clambered up, grasping a branch, ducking under old roseships, twigs in my hair.

Scattered against the bank was a hidden treasury of glints, a carpet of satiny circles. Pennywort, so-called because it resembles coins, but I prefer its other name, for its ever-green gathering of flesh that remembers the cord that bound us at birth: navelwort. This could be the omphalos, the very centre of everything. A fleshy pinpoint in a plant, a bodily enchantment in the hedge-world.

Up above my head, a magpie pair flew in, flicked their stark black tails one after the other and cackled out their call and return: what more will this year bring, what more?

## "From the hedge bottom where the ivy runs"

From the hedge bottom where the ivy runs
The little violet most divinely swells
& primrose that in moss clad spiney dwells
Eager to catch the smiles of early suns

Upon the dyke side early errand tells
In spite of dun hued skies that spring is near
The earliest comer of the early year
Aye silent little birds why dont ye sing
So thinks the rustic stooping down to pull

The early blossoms till his hands are full
& they do sing wood ramblers hear the sounds
Pink pink the buntings sing in little grounds
To me more sweet then when all sing together
It tells of hedgrows green & sunny weather


*John Clare (1793 – 1864)*